BENJAMIN C. YABLON
BANKRUPTCY ATTORNEY AT LAW

For individuals and families overwhelmed by de

The Bankruptcy Guide

By Benjamin C. Yablon

(303) 562-3167

Dear Reader:

Financial crises can happen to anyone. The world of consumer bankruptcy can be frightening and overwhelming.

Do yourself a favor: Stop and take a deep breath. Typically, the worst part of filing bankruptcy is figuring out your options and learning how the process works. It almost always gets better from there.

This guide is intended for individuals and families that are contemplating filing for bankruptcy protection. *The Bankruptcy Guide* is meant to be as reader friendly as possible. To that end, I have done my best to cut out legal jargon and "terms of art" used in the legal field. The result is a straightforward, accessible guide to the bankruptcy process.

Bankruptcy is governed by Federal Law, but each state handles certain aspects of the Bankruptcy Code differently. My law practice is in Colorado, so if you live in the Centennial State and need help, call me. If you live outside of Colorado and need an attorney, consider looking at your state's bar association website for a list of practitioners in your area.

The Bankruptcy Guide will help you understand how bankruptcy works, but every case is different. Knowledge is power, and the best piece of knowledge I can pass on is to hire a lawyer for your case. Filing bankruptcy on your own, known as “Pro Se” filing (sorry for the jargon), is risky in almost every case. You should be wary of document preparation services, as well. They are not lawyers and are under no legal or ethical obligation to tell you the truth!

Best wishes,
Benjamin C. Yablon
Attorney at Law

TABLE OF CONTENTS

II. *Bankruptcy Specifics*

A. Chapters of Bankruptcy – Chapters 7, 11, 12, and 13

B. Business Bankruptcy – Chapters 7 and 11

C. Bankruptcy and Divorce

D. Bankruptcy Trustee – Chapter 7

E. Bankruptcy Trustee – Chapter 13

F. Exemptions

G. Discharge

H. Objections to Discharge

I. Credit after Bankruptcy

J. Attorney Fees

K. Fee Agreement & Retainer

L. Initial Consultation Agreement & Required Notices

M. Acknowledgement of Receipt

N. Sample Creditor Stop-Contact Letter

Bankruptcy in a Nutshell

Bankruptcy and Fraud: What you must know before you file

The new bankruptcy law passed by Congress in 2005 (The Bankruptcy Reform and Abuse Prevention Act of 2005), was put into effect under the auspices of catching "abusive filings." Most people would take this to mean that it was designed to catch criminals attempting to file bankruptcy. However, the practical result of the law is to deny protection to an entire swath of the honest American public.

The key addition to the new law is called the "means test." This test looks at the six months preceding the month in which a case is filed and "annualizes" (multiplies by two) the gross income received by the individual. This includes the income resulting from the sale and liquidation of assets like cars, motorcycles, and even 401(k)'s. All this income goes into the pot and is used to force people away from Chapter 7 bankruptcy (90 days, quick and easy) and into Chapter 13 bankruptcy (5 years, low success rate).

Common criminal acts under bankruptcy statutes can involve the concealment of assets, destruction of documents, fraudulent claims, conflicts of interest, false statements, fee fixing or redistribution arrangements, and the acquisition of new debt without the intent to repay it. Falsifications on bankruptcy schedules can constitute perjury. Filing bankruptcy multiple times is not in and of itself fraud, but may create problems, depending on the state of mind of the person filing.

The United States Trustee's office was given a large budget boost under the new law. However, if the US Trustee is so busy catching "abusive" filings (i.e. those deemed to have too much money), who is looking at the actual criminals filing bankruptcy? You guessed it... no one that wasn't looking for them before the law changed.

For those out to cheat the system, the game is the same: understate your assets and use bankruptcy as another tool to move through life the wrong way. For those honest, hard-working Americans who sold everything they had to pay debts and still ended up in bankruptcy, there is a revitalized US Trustee's office filled with accountants and paralegals hired to ferret out those deemed to be "abusing" the system.

Bankruptcy fraud can be investigated by the FBI and is punishable by up to six years in Federal prison, revocation of a discharge, and a $500,000.00 fine. It is not something to take lightly.

How to Avoid Fraud

If you are in debt and considering selling assets to repay your creditors, talk to an attorney first. Debt settlement may be an alternative to bankruptcy. However, it should only be considered after vetting competent settlement experts.

Typically, debts can be settled for 50% or less of their outstanding balance, but there is a huge risk when dealing with debt collectors on your own. Selling assets before filing for bankruptcy can be a deal-killer under the new law. The money received counts as gross income and will be used by the US Trustee to force you to file a Chapter 13, when you may have qualified for a Chapter 7, based on your wages alone. Why? Because you now "make" too much money! It's an unfair and slanted law, but it is the one we must work with. Not disclosing the sale or transfer of an asset is fraud.

The main reason to use a debt settlement lawyer is the protection provided you in case a creditor claims that a payment you supposedly made in full settlement of an account was actually just a partial payment. When a lawyer has settled the debt, the next step is a lawsuit. A good settlement lawyer will have kept clear records of the transaction and will have an easy case in front of them. However, hiring a lawyer after you have settled a debt on your own and are then involved in a dispute with a creditor, will cost a small fortune. Attorneys avoid messy cases that they did not help create, unless they are being paid by the hour. Even then, there is no guarantee that the settlement documents you have will hold up in court.

If settlement is not an option and bankruptcy makes the most sense, the best thing you can do is recognize the problem early and begin planning your case with an attorney. Do not wait until a creditor has sued you. Once local debt collection law firms are involved and a wage garnishment is around the corner, your chances to adequately plan for a bankruptcy disappear.

Bankruptcy and Home Owners Associations: What you need to know

Aggressive Home Owners Associations (HOA's) have hired law firms to pursue individuals who have filed for bankruptcy protection, and they are winning. This is bad news for individuals who have purchased real estate over the last few years, using adjustable rate mortgages (ARM's). As interest rates have climbed, many home buyers have been forced to surrender their property to the bank. But that is just the beginning of the HOA nightmare.

Under Colorado law, HOA's are collecting on post-bankruptcy petition debts. Their theory is that the debt was incurred after the petition was filed and, therefore, was not discharged. Until the title actually passes back to the bank, they are successfully collecting on post-petition assessments.

So, just when you, as a consumer, think you are getting back on your feet… bam! The HOA firm comes after you with a civil suit and a potential garnishment is not far behind. "But wait… I just filed bankruptcy!" you protest. "Aren't I protected?"

No, you're not. The HOA's are successfully going after the assessments they are owed post-petition. The credit nightmare is not over for you, and credit rehabilitation is useless at this point. Forget about buying another home in the next year. It won't happen. Not with lenders running for the hills and your credit being destroyed by a debt you thought was handled in your bankruptcy.

Is there any good news? Yes, because there are a couple of ways to deal with this problem. First, if your debt is fairly small ($500 or less), the HOA is not going to pay its attorneys to chase it down. That said, the sure-fire way to deal with them is to stop making the mortgage payments *prior* to the bankruptcy being filed. Then call the bank and tell them you want to surrender the house. Ask if they will accept a deed in lieu of foreclosure. If they will, once the title passes, you are off the hook for the HOA assessments. If the bank will not accept the deed in lieu of foreclosure, do anything you can to light a fire under their foreclosure department, although this may be difficult because of the high foreclosure rate in Colorado.

After the foreclosure is complete and title has passed back to the bank, file the bankruptcy on the outstanding debt (including the HOA dues), and start rebuilding your credit. Be sure that your homeowner's insurance is being paid until the bank has title. If the house burns to the ground, the risk of loss remains yours until title has passed. And beware of signing a promissory note to make the deal go through. Such a promissory note is more than likely non-dischargeable in bankruptcy.

The bottom line: until the foreclosure on your property is complete and the redemption period has expired, you must keep a close eye on HOA assessments.

Bankruptcy and Secured Property: Why Reaffirm a Debt?

Secured property is anything purchased on which a balance is owed to the creditor, like a car, some furniture, a computer, a boat, or a house. It is sometimes called a "security," because it protects the debt for the creditor. If you default on the amount due on your secured property, the creditor can not only repossess the property, but they can then hold you responsible for the balance due on the purchase.

When you file for bankruptcy, secured property can be a major headache. In Chapter 7 liquidation bankruptcies, payments must be current or you will likely lose the collateral. In Chapter 13 bankruptcies, you can keep the collateral as long as you pay the amount due each month after the filing date of your case. The amount you were behind is repaid through the Chapter 13 plan. In the Chapter 7 context, creditors will discuss reaffirmation agreements.

Under the current bankruptcy law, creditors holding secured collateral can require you, as an individual or a couple filing together, to sign what is known as a "Reaffirmation Agreement" if you wish to retain your secured collateral. A reaffirmation agreement takes your debt outside the scope of a bankruptcy. It effectively nullifies the discharge as to the particular debt reaffirmed.

"Reaffs," as they're known, could not be required

under the old bankruptcy law. If you fell behind on your payments six months (or even a year) after your bankruptcy case was discharged, you could then surrender the property without fear of a collectable deficiency balance. Creditors would always ask you to sign a reaff because they had nothing to lose. Unfortunately, individuals not represented by attorneys often signed the reaff because they didn't understand the implications.

Whether or not you should sign a reaffirmation agreement depends on several factors. The first (and most important) is whether you will be able to continue making the payments. Simply wanting to be able to keep the property is not enough. Once your debt is reaffirmed, surrendering the property because you can't afford it is a bad option.

The creditor will take back the property and sell it, often for far less than the reaffirmed balance. The difference between what the property was sold for and the amount reaffirmed is called the "deficiency," and because the debt was reaffirmed, that deficiency is collectable. In other words, it has effectively been taken outside the scope of your bankruptcy protections.

The second factor to consider is what your income is likely to do over the remaining term of the reaffirmed agreement. If the term is relatively short and the payment is reasonable, it might be worth your while to sign the agreement. The key is to determine if your debt is likely to be a burden. If it is, then don't reaffirm.

What if you have no choice? In some cases, the only way to keep a car is to sign the reaff. You may worry that if you don't sign the agreement, your car will be repossessed. Technically, the new law gives secured creditors this right, but in practice, the last thing they want is the collateral. The creditor is in the business of collecting payments, not reselling used cars or other property. Bottom line: if you are current on your payments, a car dealer or other creditor is not going to force you to sign a reaffirmation agreement. They will ask for one, but attorneys are typically still advising clients not to sign them. After all, the agreement requires that the attorney warrant to the Court that the debtor (you) has the present and future ability to repay the debt.

The last I checked, law schools weren't issuing crystal balls, so if a creditor pushes the issue, fine. Let them take back their collateral. Allow the debt to be discharged. I help my clients get back to good credit scores within a year of filing bankruptcy. They can always buy new secured property such as a car once their FICO scores are back in the "A" category.

Bankruptcy and the Non-Filing Spouse

The Bankruptcy Reform and Abuse Prevention Act of 2005 drastically changes the way American families can file for bankruptcy protection. In many cases, only one spouse has accrued the lions' share of consumer debt and needs bankruptcy protection. Under the old law, this was not a problem. The spouse in need of protection simply submitted a bankruptcy petition for consideration, using only his or her financial information. The non-filing spouse was only affected if joint debt existed.

Things have changed. Under the new law, total household income is considered when determining what chapter of bankruptcy an individual qualifies for. If you and your spouse make over the median income or don't have enough justifiable expenses to eat up your *combined* budget, you must file a Chapter 13 bankruptcy. This involves a three- to five-year repayment plan. Gone are the days when, despite a low or no *personal* income, you can qualify for the relief of a 90-day Chapter 7 if your spouse has a high income.

The effect of the new law is to force non-filing spouses with high incomes to subsidize the filing spouse's Chapter 13 repayment plan. The non-filing spouse may not have helped accumulate any of the debt, but Congress has made it clear that he or she will have a major role in repaying it. Needless to say, this quirk of congressional intent is creating marital strife in many households.

All is not lost, however. Competent legal counsel may still be able to help families find ways to fit within the boundaries of the new law…as long as you don't wait. Emergency filings should be avoided at all costs, because they take many important options off the table. The most important thing families can do, when only one spouse needs to file, is recognize the need for a bankruptcy early and start planning.

Bankruptcy Is Not Gone, Just Forgotten

Contrary to what the credit card industry would have Americans believe, the federal bankruptcy laws are still alive and well, albeit underused. The main change in the law that took effect in October of 2005 is that it forced more people into 5-year Chapter 13 repayment plans than into straight 90-day Chapter 7 liquidations.

That said, you only have to file a Chapter 13 if you make over the median income in your state—a figure that varies by county—and have too much money left over each month. And even if you are over the median income, if you have enough justifiable expenses (typically medical), you can still file a Chapter 7.

People get into financial trouble for all kinds of reasons. Regardless of what the credit industry claims, the big four are still divorce, illness, job loss, and entrepreneurship. Financial irresponsibility accounts for less than 10% of all filings. One unintended consequence of the new law will be to discourage Americans from undertaking the daunting task of starting a small business.

Bankruptcy is not gone, just forgotten by most people who need the help. Sadly, an entire industry has sprung up that is specifically designed to feed on the fact that most people in financial trouble don't know that there is still protection. For instance, the bankruptcy law allows people to protect up to

$60,000 in home equity in Colorado; this provision has not changed under the new law. But, as a partial result of the new law, borderline predatory lenders have sprung up to help part the uninformed from their hard-earned home equity.

If you are in debt and seriously considering a refinance to pay off your credit cards, you owe it to yourself and your loved ones to know all your rights. Creditors always protect themselves. Don't forget that the law protects your interests as well!

The Bankruptcy Abuse Prevention and Consumer Protection Act (BAPCPA)

Congress likes irony. I challenge anyone to find a single provision in this law that offers "Consumer Protection." Federal bankruptcy laws have changed for the first time in more than a quarter century. The key change caused by the Bankruptcy Reform Act affects whether individuals or married people filing jointly can file under Chapter 7 or Chapter 13 of the Bankruptcy Code. Chapter 7 bankruptcy is a 90-day process that discharges all of a person's debt at once. Chapter 13, on the other hand, involves a 3- to 5-year repayment plan in which a monthly payment is made to the Bankruptcy Trustee who distributes the funds to the creditors.

The effect of the law's change will be felt most acutely by those whose income is above the median in Colorado, approximately $75,000 for a family of four. People making over the median income will no longer be eligible to file a Chapter 7; instead, they will be forced to file a Chapter 13. The court will also employ a "means" test to determine who can file under Chapter 7. Individuals that have the ability to repay 25% or more of their debts will not be eligible to file a Chapter 7. All individuals seeking bankruptcy protection will have to undergo mandatory credit counseling through a recognized credit counselor within the six months preceding the filing of the petition.

Provisions of the new law affect others, as well, especially those that have filed bankruptcy before. One of the most powerful tools used to protect individuals, the Automatic Stay, prevents creditors from commencing any type of collection activity once a petition is filed. This protection is being drastically changed for debtors that have filed before or for debtors that have had their cases dismissed because of problems with the schedules they submit to the court. The new law allows creditors to ignore the Automatic Stay if they are deemed to have received insufficient notice of the bankruptcy filing.

As of April 20th, 2005, when President Bush signed the law, individuals must have lived in their state for the two years prior to filing in order to use the exemptions of the state in which they live. If you do not meet the two year residency requirement, you must use the exemption laws of the state in which you spent the majority of the previous two years. This provision is an attempt to close the unlimited homestead exemptions of states like Florida and Texas.

The new laws are much less debtor friendly, and considerable litigation is sure to arise over the next few years as attorneys try to make sense out of the sometimes contradictory bill. Fortunately, only one provision of the new law will not be fully implemented for six months from the date President Bush signed the legislation, giving attorneys and their client's time to discuss the best way to structure their petitions.

Credit Repair, Debt Settlement, and Bankruptcy: Part 1

Bankruptcy is a difficult process under the new law. Individuals and families deemed to make too much money are forced away from a clean-cut Chapter 7 filing and into a cumbersome Chapter 13 repayment plan. Those with the means to repay their debts should do so; I am not disputing that. But the payment amount required under the Chapter 13 framework uses an artificially high income figure to determine just what monthly payment debtors are required to make. The law looks at a wage earner's gross income in determining how much "disposable" income there is, not at his or her net income. It is no wonder that so many cases are dismissed for failure to make payments.

For those able to qualify for a Chapter 7 case, there is relief in sight. But do not wait until your income goes up or a family member gives you money to survive. Find a good lawyer and file! For those contemplating Chapter 13, look elsewhere first.

Where to look? Debt settlement versus debt consolidation

The Gold Standard. Debt settlement involves direct negations between your lawyer and your creditors to arrive at a lump sum payment amount. This option avoids the bankruptcy completely and is far less damaging to your credit. The catch? You have to have at least half of your outstanding debt available for settlement. Why use a lawyer? Because an attorney tracks the paperwork and makes sure the settlement is honored. The last thing you want is to settle a debt on your own and have the creditor come back a year later claiming you still have a balance owed.

Other People's Money. Debt consolidation is typically *not* a great option. In a consolidation, you end up repaying 100% of your outstanding debt, interest on the debt, and the consolidation company's fee! The worst part is that the consolidation company takes your money at the beginning of the month, invests it on its own to make a spread, and then pays your debt at the end of the month—*late.* This means that the entire time you are in the consolidation, your credit is being further damaged. A better option (but still not the best, in my opinion) is a Chapter 13 bankruptcy case. Sometimes those who got hooked into using a consolidator will pay the company for months or years, only to be sued anyway by their creditors. At least in a Chapter 13, you have the protection of federal bankruptcy laws to keep your creditors from having this option.

How do you come up with the money to settle your debt? Borrow the money from a friend or family member who will allow you to repay it at little to no interest. If you can make that happen, you are golden. You don't have to come up with 50% of your total debt, just 50% of the account you wish to settle.

So, if you have a few large accounts, pay them off first. Then tackle the little ones.

Future Credit and Credit Repair

This process is complicated and fraught with misinformation. The bottom line: anyone can get back to a good credit score. Whether you have been through a bankruptcy, debt settlement, or just have a low credit score, credit rehabilitation should be considered. Anyone with sub-optimal credit should work to bring up his or her score. Financial health is just like physical heath. If it is ignored, it will cause problems later. Good financial health starts with a good credit score. Don't ignore it!

Credit Repair, Debt Settlement, and Bankruptcy: Part 2

You maintain your car, your home, and your body regularly… why not your credit? Like it or not, your credit score is used to make all kinds of decisions about you in today's business world. From the actual cost of your home and car insurance premiums to employment decisions by potential bosses, your credit score is used for more than determining what interest rate a bank will charge you.

The problem? Banks don't want you to know what factors the score is based upon. False information abounds. For instance, if you have a bankruptcy on your credit report, can you ever get another line of credit? Of course you can. The banks will send you offers for new credit cards the day after your case is filed. The reason? You are a good credit risk again; you can't file bankruptcy for eight years, *AND* you aren't dealing with other unsecured debt.

Good idea? No. This is not the way to rebuild your credit.

New, unsecured lines of credit do not improve your credit score. They carry a high risk of default and they are often the reason for the bankruptcy filing in the first place. They should be avoided. If you need a credit card for emergencies, fine. Other than that, steer clear of them.

The real answer(s): New relationships with different banks and diligence with your credit reports will allow you to get your credit score up in a matter of a year. In my *12 Steps to Financial Health,* this process is laid out in detail. I provide the information free of charge to all my bankruptcy clients, but they are not the only ones who can benefit from the process.

Who needs credit repair? Anyone who has negative entries on one of the three major credit union reports can benefit from credit repair. And, anyone who doesn't qualify for a bankruptcy filing and is, therefore, looking at settlement options needs a credit repair strategy.

Bottom line? Take care of your credit like you do your car. Tune it up regularly by looking over your credit reports. Every year, go to www.AnnualCreditReport.com, a *FREE* site that does not want a credit card number. While it does not give you a FICO score, it gives you a free look at what is on all three major credit bureau reports.

If there are negative items, hire someone to help you get them removed by either paying the debt in full or working out a settlement. Once the negative items are dealt with, you can move forward with credit repair.

Foreclosure and Chapter 7 Bankruptcy

There are two types of individual bankruptcies: Chapter 7 and Chapter 13. For those with enough money in their budgets, a Chapter 13 repayment plan will allow them to save their homes from foreclosure. For those without the ability to afford a repayment plan, Chapter 7 provides a very good alternative. Unfortunately, many individuals and families contemplating bankruptcy are scared off by the fact that a foreclosure will be part of the process. As a result, they delay their filing longer than is advisable and end up filing on an emergency basis to stop a wage or bank account garnishment.

If you are one of these people, your nervousness is often exacerbated by high-pressure sales tactics from real estate agents attempting to convince you that you will never again be able to buy a house after the foreclosure. If there is no equity in your home, or if the payments are too high for you to make them, a Chapter 7 liquidation makes sense. It allows you to get a fresh start and breathe more easily. And regardless of what a realtor says, a bankruptcy filing does not prevent you from buying a home again. Quite the opposite, in fact.

The key to getting a home after the bankruptcy process is your credit score. You *MUST* rehabilitate your credit if you plan to finance anything after the ten years following your bankruptcy or foreclosure. Always keep in mind that real estate agents only get paid when they sell a home. As long as the sale is complete, they are happy. The fact that you are not making any money on the deal (or may even be losing money) is irrelevant to whether or not they get paid.

Even if your home has been the subject of a foreclosure, you can get back to a good credit score within two years. The most important issue is making sure that new negative items are not showing up on your credit report after the bankruptcy is filed or after the foreclosure is complete. Bankruptcy stays on a credit report for seven to ten years, but it alone does not prevent you from getting back to a good credit score. Part of the score is based on how much unsecured debt you have. By filing for bankruptcy and discharging your debts, you may actually see your credit score go up shortly afterwards.

Another important issue to keep in mind is that it is illegal for creditors or employers to discriminate against you based on the fact that you have sought protection under the bankruptcy code. Employers who do so are subject to federal lawsuits. That said, employers and banks can look at your credit report and make a negative decision based on the information contained in it. So, if you have many open accounts and a large amount of revolving debt, it is not illegal for them to discriminate. In these circumstances, your seeking protection under the bankruptcy code can actually save your job.

The stigma associated with bankruptcy is created by the credit industry. Keep in mind they will always protect themselves, but, at some point, you must do so as well.

Is Bankruptcy Cheating?

Flat out, no! Most of the people who file bankruptcy are in need of real protection from creditors. Nothing makes the credit industry happier than being able to charge hard-working Americans high interest rates. It's about the easiest way to fatten their bottom line profits. Without the bankruptcy code as a safety valve, we would have massive social and economic upheaval. The bankruptcy code allows many Americans to get a fresh start and become productive members of society again.

A few noteworthy bankruptcy filers: Abraham Lincoln, John James Audubon, P.T. Barnum, Kim Basinger, Frank Baum, Buffalo Bill, Raymond Carver, Miguel de Cervantes, Samuel L. Clemens ("Mark Twain"), John Connally, Francis Ford Coppola, Dorothy Dandridge, Daniel Defoe, Walt Disney, Henry Ford, William Fox, Red Foxx, Zsa Zsa Gabor, Marvin Gaye, Charles Goodyear, Ulysses S. Grant, Johannes Gutenberg, M.C. Hammer, George Frideric Handel, Richard Harris, Isaac Hayes, H.J. Heinz, Don Johnson, Larry King, Robert Kiyosaki, Cyndi Lauper, George McGovern, William McKinley, Willie Nelson, Wayne Newton, Tom Petty, Rembrandt, Burt Reynolds, Mickey Rooney, Johnny Unitas, Oscar Wilde... *and on and on, the list goes.*

Certainly, you don't need to be famous to file bankruptcy. Financial crises can happen to anyone. But don't put off the decision to file because you have been shamed into believing that bankruptcy is dishonest or immoral. This is a mistake. The fact that bankruptcy has become an emergency decision for you does not mean your case can be submitted overnight. The new law forces debtors to gather a massive amount of data. If you have left yourself a few months to gather the data and pay your bankruptcy attorney in installments, things are much simpler. If you are forced to come up with the entire balance of the legal fees and gather the paper work necessary to file in a week or less, you may end up having to borrow money from friends or family members in order to move forward.

The worst case scenario involves emergency cases filed without the aid of an attorney. The only person on your side in the entire process is your lawyer. No one else is required to explain the legal consequences of anything involved in the process.

The credit industry did its best to destroy the bankruptcy system in 2005, but competent judges and lawyers nationwide are carving it out again. When the bankruptcy code was gutted in 2005, the new law was called "The Bankruptcy Abuse Prevention and Consumer Protection Act of 2005" (or "BAPCPA").

Nowhere in this document are there any provisions to protect consumers, however. It was a law designed to force individuals and families alike into a Chapter 13 debtor prison. The founders of our country would be sickened by this system.

All is not lost, however. A recent case was decided in favor of debtors. No longer will attorneys or debtors be forced to take a retirement distribution into account when determining whether or not a person's income is too high to file Chapter 7. Too bad for all the cases the US Trustee got dismissed prior to the case being decided, but at least the tide is moving back toward a more reasonable system than the one foisted on Americans by international lending institutions.

The key to the new law is for you to recognize your financial problem *early* and move forward accordingly. So, to go back to the question of whether bankruptcy is a form of cheating… the answer, once again, is a resounding *NO*. Planning with a competent lawyer to file a case is not illegal, even though some are eager to proclaim such nonsense. You'll notice that creditors always protect themselves. At some point, those faced with crushing debt must do so as well.

Life after Bankruptcy: What banks don't tell you

What happens after your bankruptcy has been discharged? How do you make sure that you are going to be able to qualify for decent interest rates on homes, cars, and even credit cards in the future? A bankruptcy stays on your credit report for seven to ten years, but you can get back to a good credit score within a year or two if you know what you're doing.

It is illegal for anyone to discriminate against you based on the fact that you have sought protection under the bankruptcy Code. However, employers and banks can look at your credit report and make a decision based on the information contained therein. Once they see the bankruptcy notation, they are not allowed to make a negative decision based *solely* on that fact. However, if your credit score has not improved, they can certainly rely on *that* fact in their decision.

As we have discussed, the best thing you can do after a bankruptcy is make sure that your credit score improves. There are several ways to accomplish this, but by far the most important is staying diligent in looking over your credit report. A bankruptcy discharge ends your legal obligation to pay on the debts that have been discharged. This does not mean, however, that all negative insertions come off your credit report; it merely means that they must be reported as discharged if they were properly included in your filling. If negative insertions are showing up on your credit report that should have been discharged in the bankruptcy, this will result in a slower credit rehabilitation process.

The worst thing that you can have happen after a bankruptcy is to have new negative items show up on your credit report. Taking out new lines of unsecured credit and not paying them on time is a killer. Some negative items may be unavoidable, like a foreclosure. But, in many cases, people file bankruptcy planning to keep their homes. For one reason or another, though, they may end up having to surrender the home after the bankruptcy discharge has been entered, and the foreclosure begins. This is not the end of the world, but it will slow down the time it takes to rebuild your credit.

Credit reporting bureaus have special procedures for disputing negative items on their reports. I provide my clients with sample letters to use during this process that effectively disputes the incorrect items. If information cannot be verified with a creditor, or can be shown to have been discharged in a bankruptcy, it must be accurately reported.

Once all the negative items are reported accurately, it is time for the next important phase: new relationships with different banks. This step can be the most important one you take. Having a new bank add positive items to your credit report will show the credit world that you are once again worthy of competitive interest rates. The key to remember is that it is up to *YOU* to get your credit score restored. How? By staying diligent and being pro-active at all times.

The Perils of Pro Se Bankruptcy and "Free" Consultations

Prior to the passage of the Bankruptcy Reform Act of 2005, filing a bankruptcy *pro se* (without a lawyer) was relatively simple. Not any more! The disclosures required for a Chapter 7 bankruptcy petition have at least tripled. This fact is not lost on corporations that produce and sell do-it-yourself legal packets. The not-so-innovative tactic used by these companies is to send customers to attorneys who offer a "free consultation," before they complete the bankruptcy filing on their own. Unfortunately, this can lead to disastrous outcomes.

Under the new law, if you fail to undergo credit counseling, submit six months of pay stubs, and account for all additional income over the last six months (including income from gifts, retirement disbursals, stock sales, etc.), your case will be dismissed or converted to another bankruptcy chapter. If this happens, you may lose the ability to receive a Chapter 7 discharge for six months. A new case must be filed and entirely new paperwork submitted.

An attorney providing a "free consultation" is not required to give you this information. Until you retain an attorney, no attorney-client relationship and no protection for you or your petition exists. Furthermore, while this "free consultation" attorney is required to evaluate a particular situation on your do-it-yourself legal filing, he may miss many other pertinent or important details. These are the very details the new law forces judges to consider when dismissing a case… possibly *your* case. Free advice can turn out to be the most expensive advice you ever receive.

You can avoid most of the pitfalls created by the new law by hiring a competent attorney to prepare your bankruptcy petition. The money spent on a professional who is in your corner is miniscule compared to the financial and emotional hardship of having a bankruptcy "dismissed" or "converted." That said, paying legal bills is typically very difficult for individuals and families already strapped for cash. This, however, is *still* not the place to save what money you have!

The best strategy is to cut back on other expenses or get help from a friend or family member. The money you borrow can be repaid after the bankruptcy (under no condition can it be repaid *before* the case is filed). Once bankruptcy is a real option for you, your payments to creditors should stop. This typically frees up some money with which legal representation can be purchased.

<u>The bottom line</u>: Recognize that a bankruptcy is a very real solution to your financial problems. Make the decision sooner, rather than later, and take charge. If you time your filing properly, you can avoid many of the dangers of the new law. Most attorneys

will take payments over time, allowing you to refer your creditors to them while your case is being prepared. This keeps the creditors away and allows you to focus on the issues you can control.

Bankruptcy Specifics

Chapters of Bankruptcy – Chapters 7, 11, 12, and 13

The Bankruptcy Guide is designed for individuals and families that need to file bankruptcy, so Chapters 11 (Business Bankruptcy Reorganization) and 12 (Family Farmer Bankruptcy) are not covered here. However, a discussion of small business bankruptcy filing under Chapter 7 is examined.

Bankruptcy Process – Chapter 7

Means Testing

The "Means Test," sometimes called the "Mean Test" because of how unfair it can be, is the test used to determine who gets to file for Chapter 7 bankruptcy and who is required to go through a repayment plan under Chapter 13. (One important thing to note here: if the majority of your debt is business debt, you are not required to undergo the means test. Refer to the section below on Business Chapter 7 Bankruptcy.)

The Means Test looks at the last six months of household income to determine who is eligible for Chapter 7 relief. Chapter 7 bankruptcy is a 90-day process that wipes out all of your unsecured debt in one shot. Chapter 13 bankruptcy involves a five year repayment plan in which some portion of your unsecured debt is repaid. The amount repaid in Chapter 13 depends on several factors and is discussed in more detail below.

Eligibility for Chapter 7 relief is based on whether or not your household earns less than the statewide median income. In Colorado, the cut-off for an individual to file Chapter 7 bankruptcy is about $47,000 per year. The median income increases, the larger your household is. So for a family of four, the cut-off in Colorado is about $78,000 per year. If you make more than the median income, you may be required to file Chapter 13 bankruptcy and repay a portion of your debt.

Credit Counseling

Before you can file a bankruptcy under Chapter 7 or 13, you must complete a credit counseling course. The class can be taken online. The company I refer my clients to is www.startfreshtoday.com. The certificate expires every 180 days, so if you take it, and then have some kind of delay in filing your case, you will have to take it a second time.

Submission to the Court

Once a bankruptcy is filed under Chapter 7 the process takes about 90 days from start to finish. As soon as the case is filed, an Automatic Stay is issued. The Stay is an order from the bankruptcy court that stops all collection activity. Creditors can only commence their collection actions with the judge's permission. This is nearly impossible to get for creditors with unsecured claims without proving that some kind of fraud took place. Mortgage companies can get relief from the Stay Order if you are behind on your payments in a Chapter 7 case. (It is for this reason that Chapter 13 sometimes makes more sense, as discussed below.)

There is one court date set out about 30 days from the filing of the case. The hearing is in front of a bankruptcy trustee, not a judge. It is very rare to see the judge at all in a Chapter 7 filing. The 341 Meeting of Creditors, as it is known, must be held within 45 days of filing. The bankruptcy trustee is appointed by the court to administer the case.

They are not on your side; they are basically in place to make sure the *creditors* are being treated fairly. The trustee has the power to have your case thrown at and your discharge order revoked if you don't comply with their requests. For this reason alone, you should have a lawyer advising you. Only your lawyer is on your side in this process. The trustee's job is to confirm your identity at court by looking at your photo ID and social security card. He is also in place to seize and sell non-exempt property. The trustee gets to keep 15% of whatever is collected, so he is highly motivated to find and liquidate non-exempt assets (like gold bars in your backyard!) for the benefit of your creditors.

In some cases, the United States Trustee's office, a different entity altogether from the bankruptcy trustee, will audit a Chapter 7 filing to determine if the debtor(s) are in fact eligible for relief under Chapter 7 or if they should have filed Chapter 13. The US Trustee has 60 days from the date of filing to either ask for more time to determine if they are going to audit a case, or to actually file a challenge to the filing. If it is determined that the Chapter 7 eligibility requirements were not met, the case can always be converted to Chapter 13.

This is not a criminal proceeding; it is more akin to an IRS audit. The US Trustee does, however, have the power to bring criminal charges against people that have abused the bankruptcy code. (There is more information on this in the first chapter of this book.)

Both Democrats and Republicans voted for the 2005 reform of the bankruptcy code. It was claimed by lawmakers that reform was necessary to address widespread fraud. This was not—and is not—my experience. But we are stuck with this new law and its Mean Test.

A discharge of your debts is available once every 8 years. If you are not eligible to file Chapter 7 because you already received a discharge, you can file Chapter 13. A discharge is available in a Chapter 13 as long as 4 years have passed between the filing of the Chapter 13 and the discharge in the Chapter 7.

Bankruptcy Process – Chapter 13

If you don't qualify for Chapter 7 because of your income, you can still seek protection under Chapter 13. In some cases, Chapter 13 may, in fact, be a better option. For example, if you are behind on your house or car payments but have decent income, Chapter 13 will allow you to cure the missed payments over time and take away your creditors legal right to foreclose on a house or repossess a car. If your income is under the statewide median income applicable to your household size, you are eligible for a three-year repayment plan rather than a mandatory five-year plan.

Chapter 13 is similar to Chapter 7 in many ways. The same exemptions apply to both chapters. Exemptions are items of property that the trustee cannot seize and sell to pay off your debt, such as clothes, jewelry, cars, houses, etc. However, in Chapter 13, if you do have non-exempt property, like the bars of gold buried in your yard that I just referred to, you can buy them back through the repayment plan. (If you have bars of gold in your yard you may need to look at debt settlement instead of bankruptcy!)

Once a Chapter 13 is filed, there is a "341 Meeting of Creditors" set out about 30 days, just like in a Chapter 7. The trustee in the Chapter 13 checks your ID and social security card to confirm your identity and asks the same routine questions. In a Chapter 13 case, however, there is also a Confirmation Hearing set out about a month from the 341 Meeting of Creditors. At this hearing, the judge may give his or her sanction to the Plan of Reorganization that has been submitted.

Cases in Colorado are rarely confirmed on the first shot, however. There are nearly always objections filed by the Chapter 13 trustee or by creditors. The objections can usually be resolved by the filing of an Amended Plan of Reorganization. In this case, the first Confirmation Hearing results in the issuance of an Order Denying Confirmation of the Plan, and another Confirmation Hearing is set for a few weeks down the road.

Once a Chapter 13 case is confirmed, you are protected from your creditors as long as you make your monthly payments. The Confirmation Order is a big deal. It is considered a final order of the court, and as such, is non-appealable by your creditors. Unless you have failed to list something relevant to the case (like the gold bars), you are safe from creditor harassment and lawsuits.

Debt Limit

As of 2012, in Chapter 13 bankruptcy, you can not have more than $336,900 in unsecured debt or $1,010,650 in secured debt (total debt not to exceed $1,347,550). If your debt exceeds the limit, you are not allowed to file Chapter 13. If your income then precludes you from filing Chapter 7, as well, you are forced to look at Chapter 11. This is very rare, but it does happen. The complexity of Chapter 11 and 12 bankruptcies are beyond the scope of this guide.

Bankruptcy Process – Chapters 11 and 12

As stated above, the process of filing bankruptcy under Chapters 11 or 12 is beyond the scope of this guide, and as such, will not be covered.

Business Bankruptcy – Chapters 7 and 11

Chapter 11 bankruptcy is not covered here, but Chapter 7 for a small business is. You may have the option of filing a business bankruptcy and not even know it. The test is pretty simple. If the majority of your debt is business debt, then you are not required to undergo the means testing analysis. You are considered a "non-consumer" bankruptcy filer. Only "consumer debtors" are required to undergo the means testing analysis.

This can be a huge relief for people that were caught up in the real estate meltdown or have been forced to personally guarantee the debts of a small business. I have had many clients whose household income would have been too high to file Chapter 7 bankruptcy as consumer debtors but were still able to move ahead with a non-consumer Chapter 7 filing because of the nature of their debts.

When making the determination as to whether or not you are able to file as a non-consumer debtor, you must factor in all your debts, including your mortgage. Because the mortgage is often the largest debt a person has, this may limit their ability to qualify as a non-consumer filer.

Bankruptcy and Divorce

Some debts are non-dischargeable, like child or spousal support and court ordered fines. (You can't discharge parking tickets… sorry!)

A major change in the 2005 law impacts how debts are treated in bankruptcy after a divorce judge has apportioned them amongst the divorcing parties. Even though the debt may be a credit card that could have been discharged in bankruptcy, if the divorce judge orders one spouse to pay the credit card debts of the other, that debt is now non-dischargeable in bankruptcy. However, if both parties to the divorce end up filing separate bankruptcies, this provision does not apply. For this reason, it often makes sense to explore filing a joint bankruptcy before filing for divorce.

Bankruptcy Trustee – Chapter 7

The Chapter 7 trustee is appointed by the bankruptcy court to administer the case. They are typically lawyers, but they do not have to be. In Colorado, all of the trustees are lawyers. The trustee's job is to collect non-exempt property, liquidate it, and pay off some of your debts. If the trustee cannot locate enough non-exempt property (because you don't have any, not because you hid it!), they file what is known as a "no asset report." This is typically the end of their involvement in the case.

The bankruptcy trustee is separate from the US Trustee (who has oversight over who is eligible to file Chapter 7 among other things). The trustee's job is to conduct the 341 Meeting of Creditors. At the 341 Meeting, the trustee must be provided a valid state-issued photo ID and proof of your social security number. In addition, he is required to have a copy of your previous year's tax return sent to him ten days before the hearing is conducted. Failure to provide the information to which he is entitled can result in a dismissal of your case.

All trustees are a little different, but for the most part, they are professional and decent people. They are not there to beat up on you; they are there to do a very specific job. So, the easier you make their job, the more pleasant they will be. For example, showing up late to the hearing, forgetting your ID, and leaving your cell phone ringer turned on will annoy them and… all for no good reason.

If you have hired a lawyer, he or she will be with you for the 341 Meeting of Creditors. For this reason alone, it is worth hiring one. Believe me, you will be setting yourself up for more stress and anxiety than you can possibly imagine by going into this process alone. Even easy cases can be nightmarish if you have not had a lawyer handle the details and help you with many of the simple things that can completely derail your case.

For example, if you file your own bankruptcy but forget to send the trustee your tax return, the trustee may file a Motion to Dismiss your case. If you have a lawyer, he or she is going to be on top of the deadlines to get the info to the trustee. If a mistake is made, your lawyer is obligated to take care of it, even if that means setting a hearing in front of the bankruptcy judge. Sometimes people without lawyers will receive tax refund money after they file bankruptcy and spend it. This is a huge, rookie mistake. The trustee is entitled to your non-exempt tax refund money. If you have already spent it, your case could get dismissed.

Bankruptcy Trustee – Chapter 13

The Chapter 13 trustee is similar to the Chapter 7 trustee in many ways. The key difference between the two chapters is the bankruptcy plan that is submitted in Chapter 13. The plan explains to the court and to creditors how you intend to repay your debt and must be supported by bank statements and paycheck stubs. The Chapter 13 trustee's job is to satisfy what is known as the "best interests of the creditors test." This is fairly self-explanatory. The trustee is there to make sure your monthly payments are what they are supposed to be, based on your income.

Plan Payments

In a Chapter 13 bankruptcy, you are required to pay in 100% of your "disposable income." Your disposable income is calculated either by using the last six months of financial data, or your current month's income, if the circumstances warrant it. Most typically, your payments are based on the last six months of data calculated into the Means Test.

Exemptions

Almost everything you can think of is protected under the bankruptcy code. It's protected under what are called "Exemptions." Your clothing, jewelry, house wares, equity in your cars, and equity in your home are all protected and not subject to seizure by the trustee appointed to your case. The purpose of the bankruptcy code is not to leave you penniless on the street.

That said, there are specific items that are considered non-exempt that you have to turn over to the trustee. Things like bars of gold buried in your yard are non-exempt. You have to dig them up and give them to the trustee.

On the day your case is filed with the court, your petition must list all of the items in your possession. This is done on what is known as Schedule B of the petition. The exemptions you claim in your property listed on Schedule B are disclosed on Schedule C of the petition. When valuing the items you own, you do not list the price that you paid for the items; instead, use the value of the item in its current condition on the date of filing. This is known as "liquidation value" and is typically quite a bit less than what you paid.

Discharge

About 90 days after a Chapter 7 bankruptcy is filed, the judge will issue a Discharge Order. This judicially liquidates all your debt, both secured and unsecured. The Discharge can be thought of in two ways: a General Discharge of debt and a Specific Discharge of debt.

Some debts are considered non-dischargeable, which means that they survive the bankruptcy and are still collectable after the general Discharge Order has been entered. Debts considered non-dischargeable include things like student loans (unless an extreme hardship is proven through an adversary proceeding), most taxes, court ordered fines (for things like DUI), and child or spousal support.

Objections to Discharge

Creditor lawsuits, known as "Adversary Proceedings," can derail your bankruptcy. If a creditor believes that you incurred a debt without the intent to repay it, they can sue you inside your bankruptcy in a process known as an Adversary Proceeding (also known as an "AP").

Depending on the facts of the case, you may choose to defend against the AP, or you may simply try to settle the case with the creditor directly. Either way, you are dealing with a very serious set of litigation parameters akin to any federal litigation. Defending against an AP on your own is nearly impossible. The rules of procedure are complex and the judges take them seriously. Failure to follow the guidelines in the AP process can easily result in a victory for your creditor without their even having to discuss the merits of the case.

Typically the key element in a creditor's decision-making process as to whether to bring an AP case against you or not revolves around the timing of the debt in question. For example, if you meet with a bankruptcy lawyer and then go out and take a large cash advance on your credit card, it is pretty clear that you did not have the intent to repay the debt. As such, the creditor from which you borrowed the money would be on very strong ground to bring an AP against you... and win. However, if you didn't know you were going to file bankruptcy, had not yet met with a lawyer, and used your credit card to fix your car, you might still end up getting sued. Based upon the fact that you did plan to repay the debt, though, you may be able to defend against the AP.

Bottom line: If you think bankruptcy may be in your future, stop incurring any debt until you speak with a lawyer. Once bankruptcy is a real option, you stop making new charges, but you also typically stop making the minimum payments, as well. In so doing, there should be enough money in your budget to cover the necessities of life without reliance on your credit cards.

Credit after Bankruptcy

All is not lost! I help my clients get back to high credit scores after their bankruptcy. The method for repairing your credit is fairly simple and basically involves auditing your credit reports post-bankruptcy to make sure the items discharged in the case are not reporting as "open negative" accounts. The combination of monitoring your credit reports and working through a proven strategy to build relationships with new banks typically means that in a period of six to twelve months, you are back to a high credit score.

Attorney Fees

Attorney fees are paid up-front in Chapter 7. In Chapter 13, there is usually an up-front fee and then other fees and costs are paid though the plan of repayment sanctioned by the court.

Remember, you get what you pay for. You wouldn't want a cut-rate surgeon operating on you, so don't trust cut-rate lawyers. They can end up costing you a lot more in the long run by overlooking key details of your case. That said, be on the look out for lawyers charging way too much. The typical range of fees in Denver, Colorado for a simple Chapter 7 bankruptcy is $2,000.

FEE AGREEMENT & RETAINER

Jane R. and John Q. Smith:

Thank you for retaining Benjamin C. Yablon, PC to represent you. I appreciate your confidence and will proceed faithfully and diligently on your behalf.

Please sign this document as your approval and agreement with the terms of my representation. If any term is unclear, please ask for additional explanation.

For our joint benefit, I have found it best to have a full understanding of fees and costs. With regard to the above referenced matter, we have agreed that I will represent you in Chapter 7 or 13 bankruptcy. The fee schedule is as follows:

Chapter 7 or 13 base rate
$ 1,500.00

Separate Means Test Data Entry
$ __________

Joint filing (+200)
$ 200.00

Hold case more than 90 days
$ __________

Chapter 13 Plan (Chapter 13 only) (+1,000)
$ __________

US Trustee bubble case objection (+ 750 only if actually audited) $ __________

Litigation of contested matter, including UST motion to dismiss $ 250.00/hour

Vehicle Cram Down (+200 + 100 per vehicle)
$ __________

Asset case with non-exempt property
$ __________

More than 20 creditors (+250)
$ __________

More than 30 creditors (+300)
$__________
Time Share Surrender (+200)
$__________
Real Estate Surrender (+300)
$__________
Taxes (+150)
$__________
Ft. Collins or Colorado Springs (+150)
$__________
Motion to Void Lien (+500)
$__________
Business Disclosures (+500)
$__________
Emergency filing (+500)
$__________

Court filing fee (+300)
$ 300.00

Total due prior to filing: $ 2,000.00

Chapter 13 only, paid through plan: ($1,000.00 not to exceed $10,000.00)

This amount includes costs for copies, postage, and faxes associated with the administration of your bankruptcy case.

The initial consultation, file drop-off and review, and signing session are all included in the base rate. Additional consultations are available at a charge of $100.00 per half-hour meeting. Please call my answering service at (303) 562-3167 to schedule your file drop-off or additional consultation.

Either Benjamin C. Yablon or an attorney associate will assist you with the file drop-off and review, signing session, or 341 Meeting of Creditors.

This fee agreement expires six months from the date of signing. Further, failure to return all the required documents together will result in a $300.00 charge to sort and re-file documents submitted after the main packet.

The fee agreement expires upon confirmation of a Chapter 13 Plan. (Provision applies to Chapter 13 cases only.)

Bubble cases are cases in which an individual's income is close to or above the median in Colorado. In such cases the US Trustee attempts to "pop" the debtor out of Chapter 7 by requesting documentation for each monthly expense incurred over the last six months. Even when this documentation is provided, it may not be enough to satisfy the objection because the US Trustee can object to amounts spent that exceed the IRS guidelines for that particular expense. Bubble cases include cases that have been "timed" in order to fall within the median income.

Bubble cases that draw objections from the US Trustee will result in an additional $500 charge if Benjamin C. Yablon, PC is to answer said objection. This clause in no way guarantees that a US Trustee objection can be overcome by this office. It is incumbent upon the client to provide precise documentation in accordance with the US Trustee's request. The documentation must be provided to this office for inspection and delivery to the US Trustee within ten days.

My fee is earned as follows: ½ upon initial consultation(s), ¼ upon review of the Client's particular circumstances in light of the prevailing law, ¼ upon the first dispensation of any advice related to asset retention and/or exemption maximization. Upon the Client's approval (by signatures) of the Petition, attorney will appear at the first scheduled 341 Meeting of Creditors on behalf of the Client *pro bono publico*. Funds provided to attorney may be considered earned upon receipt if the above criteria have been met.

Chapter 13 Only: All time spent on Chapter 13 cases, including emails, phone calls, consultations, court hearings, correspondence with opposing counsel, correspondence with trustees, correspondence with court clerks, and the filings of amended Chapter 13 Plans, Pleadings and Schedules, will be itemized and paid in addition to the fees above. An itemized bill will be submitted to the bankruptcy court for approval upon confirmation of Chapter 13 Plan. **Additional charges assessed in Chapter 13 cases are not paid by the client directly; they are paid out of Chapter 13 Plan payments.**

Some taxes are dischargeable. An outside firm called "Tax Compromises" may need to be consulted to determine if your case qualifies. Client(s) agree to pay the cost of hiring Tax Compromises to obtain and review your tax transcripts to make said determination.

Client(s) agree that their case will be submitted for filing at my discretion. Depending on my case load, I will need at least a four-week window in which to file your case. This fee agreement does not include (1) criminal matters, whether or not they relate to debt; (2) negotiations with creditors (including reaffirmation agreements and real estate negotiations); and (3) contested matters. Historically, contested matters happen in only about 1 in 100 cases. They involve situations in which you are accused of defrauding a creditor, such as charging a lot of money just prior to filing, or purposely charging a debt when you know you are going to file bankruptcy. This includes US Trustee audits. In these cases, there is a separate trial, which is in addition to the bankruptcy. For such matters with respect to which I agree to represent you, attorney fees are billed at an hourly rate. Senior attorney fees are billed at $300.00 per hour, Associate attorney fees are billed at $225.00. Paralegal services are billed at $140.00 per hour. Additional attorney fees are also charged on an hourly basis, including travel time in the event clients do not appear for the first scheduled 341 Meeting of Creditors.

I will make every effort to confer with you prior to any large expenditure for specialized services that may be needed, such as: depositions, investigative services, and appraisals of personal or real property. I reserve the right to request advance payment of any such large expenditures if I deem it appropriate.

In the event additions of creditors or other changes are required to your filing due to information that was provided after the filing of the bankruptcy, a $150.00 fee will be charged for the work required by the firm and the court's filing fee. You agree to get all information in before the filing of the documents with the court. You also understand that if there is a "change of mind" or if, at any time for any reason, no further legal services are desired, the attorney fees shall still be due and payable as agreed upon for services performed thus far. You agree to this charge even if you do not refer creditor calls.

If the arrangements set forth above meet with your approval, please sign and date in the spaces provided. I look forward to the opportunity to be of service to you at this difficult time. Should you have any questions concerning the fee arrangements or the parameters of my representation, please feel free to call me.

The use of Electronic Mail (email) to communicate with you about your case is expressly allowed. **Your email address**

is ____________________________________.

I/We agree that Attorney is <u>not</u> required to file my/our Bankruptcy Petition until such time as I/We have produced **<u>ALL</u>** of the documents that are applicable to my/our case, notwithstanding the fact that I/We may have a pending garnishment, home foreclosure, repossession, levy, etc. **<u>and</u>** given Attorney sufficient time to analyze the documents in order to prepare a bankruptcy, if applicable.

I/We understand, agree, and have been advised that any and all information and documentation provided by Me/Us to Attorney may be discoverable and might be examined by the Trustee in my case, the United States Trustee, the Bankruptcy Court, and possibly creditors pursuant to 11 U.S.C. §342(b)(2)(B).

I/We understand, agree and have been advised that we must provide complete, accurate, and truthful information and documentation. A person who knowingly and fraudulently conceals assets or makes false oath or statement under penalty of perjury in connection with a case under Title 11 shall be subject to fine, imprisonment, or both.

I/We agree that:

- ☐ I/We will produce all of the documents together at one time and not piecemeal.
- ☐ I/We will not fax the documents to Attorney and will only mail them or bring them in.
- ☐ I/We will not communicate important or material documentation or information orally to Attorney.
- ☐ I/We understand that Attorney Yablon will not sign reaffirmation agreements.

I look forward to representing you through this difficult process. Please sign below to signal your understanding and acceptance of the foregoing.

Signed:

____

Benjamin C. Yablon, Esq.

APPROVED AND ACCEPTED:

Client **Date** **Spouse** **Date**

INITIAL CONSULTATION AGREEMENT AND REQUIRED NOTICES

Please Note**:** ***These documents and disclosures are required by legislation adopted by Congress in 2005, after intense lobbying by the credit industry. In my opinion, they are designed to scare and intimidate good people who have had bad things happen to them, and need debt relief. These Notices are based on the false assumption that all people who consider bankruptcy relief are dishonest. Please rest assured—so long as you are honest and meet the requirements set out under the law, you are entitled to debt relief. We can guide you through all the requirements of filing for bankruptcy, as long as you provide us with accurate and complete information.***

Today, I had an initial consultation with Benjamin C. Yablon, P.C. (the "Firm"). I was advised that the Firm is a debt relief agency as defined in the Bankruptcy Abuse Prevention and Consumer Protection Act of 2005 ("BAPCPA"), and that it helps people file for relief under the bankruptcy code.
The Firm provides the following services at the initial consultation:

- A description of the relief available and the benefits and the risks of filing for bankruptcy under sections 7, 11, 12 and 13 of the Bankruptcy Code.
- An analysis, based on the information and documents provided by me, if any, of my income, expenses, assets, and liabilities. This analysis is only preliminary, since the Firm does not have all of the information and documents that will be required to fully evaluate my situation.
- If it has appeared from this analysis that bankruptcy may be an appropriate remedy for me, a discussion of the information and documents I will need to provide the Firm. If it has appeared from today's analysis that bankruptcy may not be an appropriate remedy for me, a discussion of other possible alternatives.

I have been informed and agree that the Firm will not provide any services or bankruptcy assistance to me at this time, other than specifically stated in this Agreement. It is understood that the Firm will not provide any other legal services to me and will not file bankruptcy for me unless and until the Bankruptcy Questionnaire has been completed, all documents and information requested have been provided, and I have received a certification and budget analysis from an approved credit counseling agency. Should I wish the Firm to provide additional services, including the filing of bankruptcy, I will sign a separate retainer agreement detailing such services and their cost.

BAPCPA REQUIRED NOTICE NO. 1 (§ 342(b)(1) and 527(a)(1) of the Bankruptcy Code) PURPOSES, BENEFITS AND COSTS OF BANKRUPTCY

This discussion is intended only as a brief overview of the types of bankruptcy. You should not decide whether or not to file for bankruptcy relief solely on this information. Bankruptcy law is complex, and there are many considerations that must be taken into account in making the determination whether or not to file. Anyone considering bankruptcy is encouraged to make a decision only after seeking the advice and assistance of an experienced bankruptcy attorney.

To put it bluntly, bankruptcy is a legal way to avoid paying people what you owe them. Bankruptcy has biblical antecedents, however. Look at the "Jubilee Year" and the forgiveness of debt in Leviticus 25. (For a more detailed discussion, ask us for a copy of the article, "The Bible and Bankruptcy.") Since there is no Jubilee Year today, in many situations, bankruptcy is the only way that you can keep your home from foreclosure, your car from repossession, your possessions other from auction, and creditors from making your life miserable. When a person is discharged in bankruptcy, he or she is relieved from liability for most debts incurred before the bankruptcy was filed and protected from future collection of those debts. The purpose of bankruptcy is to give you a "fresh start," and the bankruptcy code is interpreted by the courts to give effect to these words.

Types of Bankruptcy

The Bankruptcy Code is divided into chapters. The chapters that usually apply to consumers are Chapter 7, where most (or all) of your debt is wiped out, and Chapter 13, which involves a repayment plan.

In most cases, once you file your case, the "Automatic Stay" immediately goes into effect. The Automatic Stay means that a bankruptcy filing automatically stops, or "stays," and brings to a halt most lawsuits, repossessions, foreclosures, evictions, garnishments, attachments, utility shut-offs, and debt collection harassment. Generally, creditors cannot take any further action against you or your property without permission from the Bankruptcy Court.

Chapter 7. Chapter 7 is designed for people who are having financial difficulties and are not able to repay their debts. Under the changes to the Bankruptcy Code that took effect October 17, 2005, you can usually qualify for a Chapter 7 if your average gross monthly income for the last six months is below your state's Median Income; your gross income, less certain expenses, is below your state's Median Income; or you can show "special circumstances" that would allow you to qualify for Chapter 7. The filing fee for a Chapter 7 is $274.

Under Chapter 7, you can usually exempt, or keep, most or all of your assets under Maryland law, or, if you have not lived in Maryland for the past two years, under the state's exemption law that applies to your case. Most retirement accounts and pensions are also exempt. Secured property, normally your car and house, may not have any net equity, in which case you can keep it as well. The trustee liquidates most non-exempt property and uses the proceeds to pay your creditors according to priorities of the Bankruptcy Code.

Once your Chapter 7 case is over, you receive a Discharge. The discharge prevents your creditors from taking any steps to try to collect their unsecured debt. They cannot call you, write you, sue you, or take any steps that could be considered an attempt to collect debt. If you want to keep property that has a lien on it, you must keep your payments current and may be required to reaffirm your debt. Some debts cannot be discharged. Typical examples are child support, alimony, and other domestic support obligations, some taxes, student loans, criminal restitution, and debts for death or personal injury caused by operating vehicles while intoxicated with alcohol or drugs.

Chapter 13. Chapter 13 is a valuable tool that lets you catch up overdue mortgage or car payments, taxes and domestic support obligations. It also applies where you have the ability to repay some or all of your debts over time. You must have less than $307,675 in unsecured debt (such as credit cards and doctor's bills) and less than $922,975 in secured debt (such as mortgages and car loans) to qualify for Chapter 13. The filing fee for a Chapter 13 is $189.00.

Under Chapter 13, you keep all of your property, both exempt and non-exempt, as long as you resume making your regular payments on secured debt and keep current under the repayment plan that you propose. A repayment plan can last for up to five years. After finishing your payments, most of your unsecured debts are discharged.

Chapter 11. Chapter 11 is designed primarily for business reorganization, but is also available to consumer debtors. Its provisions are quite complex. In the vast majority of cases, Chapter 11 is unnecessary and too expensive for most consumer debtors. The filing fee for Chapter 11 is $1,039.00.

Chapter 12. Chapter 12 lets family farmers repay their debts over a period of time and is, in many ways, similar to a Chapter 13. The filing fee for a Chapter 12 is $239.

Credit Counseling. Reputable credit counselors can advise you on managing your money and your debts. They may also be able to develop a plan to repay your debts. Unfortunately, many credit counselors are not reputable and charge high fees and contributions that will cause you to fall deeper into debt and damage your credit rating. Furthermore, many misrepresent their non-profit status and/or their affiliations with religious or charitable organizations, and are little more than collection agents for the credit card companies.

Under the changes to the Bankruptcy Code that took effect October 17, 2005, you are required to take two short credit counseling courses: one before you file bankruptcy and one after you have filed. We will refer you to a reputable credit counselor who has been approved by the United States Trustee Department for these courses.

BAPCPA REQUIRED NOTICE NO. 2 (§ 527(a)(2) of the Bankruptcy Code)
NOTICE OF MANDATORY DISCLOSURE TO CONSUMERS WHO CONTEMPLATE FILING BANKRUPTCY

***Please Note*: These Notices are required by legislation adopted by Congress in 2005, after intense lobbying by the credit industry. In our opinion, these notices are designed to scare and intimidate good people who have had bad things happen to them, and need debt relief. These Notices are based on the false assumption that all people who consider bankruptcy relief are dishonest. Please rest assured—so long as you are honest and meet the requirements set out under the law, you are entitled to debt relief. We can guide you through all the requirements of filing bankruptcy, as long as you provide us with accurate and complete information.**

1. All information that the assisted person is required to provide during a case under this title must be complete, accurate and truthful.
2. All assets and all liabilities are required to be completely and accurately disclosed in the documents filed to commence the case, and the replacement value of each asset as defined in section 506 must be stated in those documents, where requested, after reasonable inquiry to establish such value.
3. Current monthly income, the amounts specified in section 707(b)(2) and, in a case under Chapter 13 of this title, disposable

income (determined in accordance with section 707(b)(2)), are required to be stated after reasonable inquiry; and
4. Information that an assisted person provides during their case may be audited pursuant to this title, and failure to provide such information may result in dismissal of the case under this title or other sanction, including a criminal sanction.

BAPCPA REQUIRED NOTICE NO. 3 (§ 342(b)(2) of the Bankruptcy Code)
FRAUD & CONCEALMENT PROHIBITED

If you decide to file bankruptcy, it is important that you understand the following:

1. Some or all of the information you provide in connection with your bankruptcy will be filed with the bankruptcy court on forms or documents that you will be required to sign and declare as true under penalty of perjury.
2. A person who knowingly and fraudulently conceals assets or makes a false oath or statement under penalty of perjury in connection with a bankruptcy case shall be subject to fine, imprisonment, or both.
3. All information you provide in connection with your bankruptcy case is subject to examination by the Attorney General.

BAPCPA REQUIRED NOTICE NO. 4 (§ 527(b) of the Bankruptcy Code)
IMPORTANT INFORMATION ABOUT BANKRUPTCY ASSISTANCE SERVICES

<u>Please Note</u>: These Notices are required by legislation adopted by Congress in 2005, after intense lobbying by the credit industry. In our opinion, these notices are designed to scare and intimidate good people who have had bad things happen to them, and need debt relief. These Notices are based on the false assumption that all people who consider bankruptcy relief are dishonest. Please rest assured—so long as you are honest and meet the requirements set out under the law, you are entitled to debt relief. We can guide you through all the requirements of filing bankruptcy, as long as you provide us with accurate and complete information.

If you decide to seek bankruptcy relief, you can represent yourself, you can hire an attorney to represent you, or you can get help in some localities from a bankruptcy petition preparer who is not an attorney. THE LAW REQUIRES AN ATTORNEY OR BANKRUPTCY PETITION PREPARER TO GIVE YOU A WRITTEN CONTRACT SPECIFYING WHAT THE ATTORNEY OR BANKRUPTCY PETITION PREPARER WILL DO FOR YOU AND HOW MUCH IT WILL COST. Ask to see the contract before you hire anyone.

The following information helps you understand what must be done in a routine bankruptcy case to help you evaluate how much service you need. Although bankruptcy can be complex, many cases are routine. An attorney can help guide you through this intricate process, making it easier and less stressful for you.

Before filing a bankruptcy case, either you or your attorney should analyze your eligibility for different forms of debt relief available under the Bankruptcy Code and which form of relief is most likely to be beneficial for you. Be sure you understand the relief you can obtain and its limitations. To file a bankruptcy case, documents called a Petition, Schedules and Statement of Financial Affairs, as well as in some cases a Statement of Intention need to be prepared correctly and filed with the bankruptcy court. You will have to pay a filing fee to the bankruptcy court. Once your case starts, you will have to attend the required first meeting of creditors where you will be questioned by a court official called a "trustee" and, much more rarely, by creditors.

If you choose to file a Chapter 7 case, you may be asked by a creditor to reaffirm a debt. You may want help deciding whether to do so. A creditor is not permitted to coerce you into reaffirming your debts. It may not be in your best interest to reaffirm a debt.

If you choose to file a Chapter 13 case in which you repay your creditors what you can afford over 3 to 5 years, you may also want help with preparing your Chapter 13 plan and with the confirmation hearing on your plan which, if held, will be before a bankruptcy judge.

If you select another type of relief under the Bankruptcy Code other than Chapter 7 or Chapter 13, you will want to find out what should be done from someone familiar with that type of relief. However, please be advised that in most cases, you will only be concerned with Chapter 7 and Chapter 13.

Your bankruptcy case may also involve litigation. You are generally permitted to represent yourself in litigation in bankruptcy court, but only attorneys, not bankruptcy petition preparers, can give you legal advice.

ACKNOWLEDGMENT OF RECEIPT

I acknowledge that I have received from Benjamin C. Yablon, P.C. a copy of all of the following documents:

1. **Consultation Agreement**
2. **Notice Mandated By Section 342(b)(1) and 527(a)(1) of the Bankruptcy Code**
3. **Notice Mandated By Section 527(a)(2) of the Bankruptcy Code**
4. **Notice Mandated By Section 527(b) of the Bankruptcy Code**
5. **Notice Mandated By Section 342(b)(2) of the Bankruptcy Code**

If my spouse was not present when I received a copy of these notices, I hereby also acknowledge receipt of said notices on behalf of my spouse and promise to provide my spouse with either a copy of these notices or the opportunity to read and review the copy I received.

Dated:
Signed: ______________________________

Signed: ______________________________

Sample Creditor Stop-Contact Letter

CLIENT USE ONLY

Dear Client:

Now that you have retained my office, you need to refer your creditors to me. Tell them you have retained an attorney and that you intend to file a Chapter 7 bankruptcy.

Give them my **Creditor Line: (303) 562-3167**.

Next, ask for their mailing or fax number and send them the letter on the following pages. You *must* send them the attached letter if you want them to stop calling you.

Once they have the letter they are on notice that you have an attorney.

If creditors won't stop calling, let them know that they are violating the Fair Debt Collection Practices Act and that you intend to pursue them. Read the highlighted portions of the law on the following pages to them so that you understand what your rights are. The key provision of the law applies to *third party* debt collectors. It prevents them from communicating with you directly once they are on notice that you have a lawyer. However, *original* creditors are still allowed to make a “reasonable” inquiry into the status of the debt.

If you can, record the conversation and let them know you are doing it. Get their personal ID number and or name and ask to speak to their supervisor. Get the information to me and we will discuss further options.

Throughout this process you must keep in mind that the bankruptcy code was rewritten by your creditors in October of 2005.

Benjamin C. Yablon PC 1444 Stuart Street, Denver Colorado 80204 (p) 303-562-3167 (f) 303-623-8223

To Whom It May Concern:

Jane R. and John Q. Smith have retained Benjamin C. Yablon, PC to prepare a Bankruptcy petition. Said petition shall be filed on or before April 15th, 2012.

Be advised that under the Fair Debt Collection Practices Act you are bound by the following:

§ 805. Communication in connection with debt collection [15 USC 1692c]

(a) COMMUNICATION WITH THE CONSUMER GENERALLY. Without the prior consent of the consumer given directly to the debt collector or the express permission of a court of competent jurisdiction, a debt collector **may not communicate** with a consumer in connection with the collection of any debt --

(1) at any unusual time or place or a time or place known or which should be known to be inconvenient to the consumer. In the absence of knowledge of circumstances to the contrary, a debt collector shall assume that the convenient time for communicating with a consumer is after 8 o'clock antemeridian and before 9 o'clock postmeridian, local time at the consumer's location;

(2) **if the debt collector knows the consumer is represented by an attorney with respect to such debt and has knowledge of, or can readily ascertain, such attorney's name and address, unless the attorney fails to respond within a reasonable period of time to a communication from the debt collector or unless the attorney consents to direct communication with the consumer**; or

(3) at the consumer's place of employment if the debt collector knows or has reason to know that the consumer's employer prohibits the consumer from receiving such communication.

(b) COMMUNICATION WITH THIRD PARTIES. Except as provided in section 804, without the prior consent of the consumer given directly to the debt collector, or the express permission of a court of competent jurisdiction, or as reasonably necessary to effectuate a post judgment judicial remedy, a debt collector may not communicate, in connection with the collection of any debt, with any person other than a consumer, his attorney, a consumer reporting agency if otherwise permitted by law, the creditor, the attorney of the creditor, or the attorney of the debt collector.

(c) CEASING COMMUNICATION. If a consumer notifies a debt collector in writing that the consumer refuses to pay a debt or that the consumer wishes the debt collector to cease further communication with the consumer, the debt collector shall not communicate further with the consumer with respect to such debt, except --

(1) to advise the consumer that the debt collector's further efforts are being terminated;

(2) to notify the consumer that the debt collector or creditor may invoke specified remedies which are ordinarily invoked by such debt collector or creditor; or

(3) where applicable, to notify the consumer that the debt collector or creditor intends to invoke a specified remedy.

If such notice from the consumer is made by mail, notification shall be complete upon receipt.

(d) For the purpose of this section, the term "consumer" includes the consumer's spouse, parent (if the consumer is a minor), guardian, executor, or administrator.

§ 813. Civil liability [15 USC 1692k]

(a) Except as otherwise provided by this section, any debt collector who fails to comply with any provision of this title with respect to any person is liable to such person in an amount equal to the sum of --

(1) any actual damage sustained by such person as a result of such failure;

(2) (A) in the case of any action by an individual, such additional damages as the court may allow, but not exceeding $1,000;

Any contact with aforementioned client(s) shall be deemed a violation of the FDCPA and may be prosecuted.

Direct any correspondence to Benjamin C. Yablon, PC at the address listed above.

Thank you,

Benjamin C. Yablon, Esq.

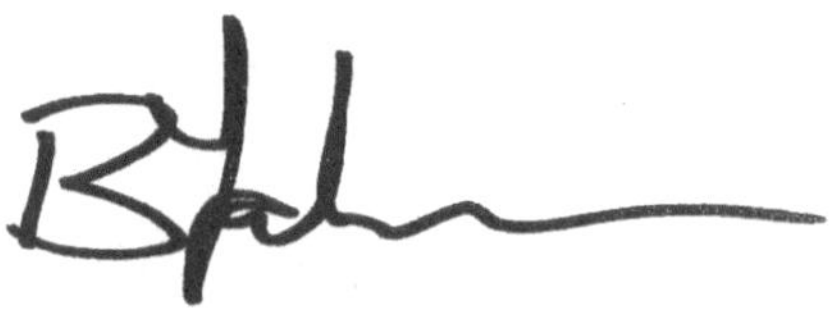

NOTE: Bankruptcy is a legal right under the US Constitution. It is governed by Federal Law. This is important because Federal Law preempts State law. What this means in practical terms is that when you file bankruptcy, any state court collection cases are stopped in their tracks. This includes home foreclosures, wage garnishments, bank levies, and any other legal action whose purpose is to collect money. The Automatic Stay issued by the Bankruptcy Judge says the following:

UNITED STATES BANKRUPTCY COURT
DISTRICT OF COLORADO

In re:	)	Case No.
xx-xxxx-xx		
	)	Case Filed
xx/xx/xxxx		
xxxxxx	)	
	)	
Debtor(s).	)	Chapter 7
	)	

NOTICE OF AUTOMATIC STAY

(Name of Creditor or Business on Whom this Notice is being Served)

(City, State, and Zip Code)

YOU ARE HEREBY NOTIFIED that the above-named debtor(s) have filed a voluntary petition in this Court. In accordance with Title 11, U.S.C. § 301, the petition constitutes an Order for Relief as of the date shown above. Additionally, pursuant to U.S.C. § 362(a), all creditors of the debtor(s) are stayed from any act, the commencement or continuation of any act, enforcement of any lien or judgment obtained against the debtor(s) or the property of their estate, or any court proceeding with respect to the enforcement of a lien or judgment against the debtor(s) or the property of their estate from and after the filing date of the bankruptcy petition, except as otherwise provided for by U.S.C. § 362(b).

Relief from the automatic stay may be sought by filing a motion in this Court pursuant to U.S.C. § 362(d).

(Signature of Pro Se Debtor or Counsel for the Debtor(s))
(Pro Se Debtor's/Counsel's Address, including City, State, and Zip Code)
(Pro Se Debtor's/Counsel's Telephone Number)

Certificate of Service

There undersigned hereby certifies that a true and correct copy of the above-captioned Notice of Automatic Stay was
[circle option that applies]:

Mailed
Hand-delivered
Sent via fax

Dated:

Signature:

Instructions:
Prepare the caption of this Notice exactly as it is shown on the original petition, inserting the case number, chapter number, and date that the petition was filed. Insert the full name and address of the party on whom this Notice is being served. Sign and complete the Pro Se debtor's/counsel's address and telephone number block. Make a copy of the Notice and deliver it to the intended party. Sign and date the Certificate of Service. File the original Notice with the Clerk of the Bankruptcy Court. Use a separate form for each party noticed. The original Notice will be "Filed-stamped" by the Clerk only after service has been completed.

After the "341 Meeting of Creditors" Post-Bankruptcy Process Begins

Reaffirmation Agreements, Pre-Discharge Education Program, Credit Rehabilitation

Reaffirmation Agreements:

Basically, a Reaffirmation Agreement puts you back on the hook for the full amount of the loan. If you default, your creditor sells the collateral and if there is a deficiency, you're liable if you reaffirmed the debt. If you just surrender the collateral and don't reaffirm it, there is NO deficiency balance you are liable for. So, if you are keeping a vehicle that is financed, then under the new bankruptcy law, there is a potential problem. Auto finance companies (not mortgage companies) now have the right to force you to either reaffirm your debt, finance it with another company, or surrender it back to the original creditor.

Here is the problem. Under the case law surrounding this area, if your lawyer signs a reaffirmation agreement, he or she is potentially personally liable on the debt, as well! Therefore, you will be hard pressed to find any lawyers that will sign these agreements. I am one such attorney. Now, your auto finance company may accept a reaffirmation agreement signed just by you, but they may not. In that case, you may have to surrender the car and get into something else. Keep in mind that your creditors, including the auto finance industry, wrote this new law. It is unfair and un-American in my opinion, but it is the law. So, the first thing you MUST do if you want to keep the car is call your auto finance company and see if they will let you keep the car by reaffirming the debt ON YOUR OWN. Again, I will not sign the agreement.

Pre-Discharge Debtor Education Program

Prior to your discharge entering, you must complete one last class. Use the same company you used to complete your first round of credit counseling. This class must be completed and filed with the Court within 45 days of your 341 Meeting of Creditors.

Once you have received the certificate, you must file it with the clerk of the US Bankruptcy Court. The clerk's office is easy to find: as you come up the stairs after you clear security, take a right and look for the clerk's office ahead on your right. You will need your case number, located on the Notice of Meeting of Creditors in order for the clerk to process your certificate.

This is the last step you must take in order to complete the bankruptcy process. If you do not submit this document in a timely manner, you will not receive your discharge. The credit rehabilitation plan I have laid out for you in this book will not have an impact on your credit score until after you have completed this last credit counseling course. (See the next section.)

12 Steps to Financial Health

This information is designed to show you the steps you need to take in order to improve your credit score. It has been designed for a person who has recently filed bankruptcy, but the techniques work equally well for someone that has not filed for bankruptcy protection. Before we get into the actual steps, you need to know a few things about the credit rating system.

First, negative items will generally appear on your credit report for 7 to 10 years from the date of the last transaction. Sometimes the last transaction can mean the last payment, rather than the last time you made a charge on the account. As a result, some negative items will stay on your credit report for more than 7 years. Court records, such as judgments, liens, and bankruptcy will remain on your credit report for up to 10 years. In Colorado, the statute of limitations to collect on a judgment is 20 years. The good news is that your positive credit notations can stay on indefinitely.

Second, it is vital to understand how your credit report will look after you file for bankruptcy protection. Many people believe that all the negative items on their credit reports (*i.e.*, 60- or 90-day late payments, repossessions, judgments, etc.) are removed by the filing of a bankruptcy petition. Unfortunately, this is not the case. The items that are on your credit reports before you file will remain on them after you file. The only important difference is that the piece of information indicating that you have filed for bankruptcy protection will be added to your credit report.

If your credit score was low before you filed bankruptcy, then the bankruptcy notation typically won't do any more damage. The bankruptcy notation may actually *help* you. For example, if you have a poor credit score, respectable income, and you have applied for a car loan, the loan will probably be denied even though you have the capacity to make the payments. This is because you have a low credit score. Even if several years have passed, the result may not change unless the negative items have been removed from the credit report.

Being in an active bankruptcy, you can be approved for an automobile or home loan once two years have passed from the date of your bankruptcy discharge. In those two years, however, your credit must be spotless, and you still need sufficient income to qualify. In this example, bankruptcy has actually improved the likelihood of loan approval.

Because the negative items remain on your credit report after you file for bankruptcy protection, the first objective is to remove as many of them as possible. Removing them is fairly straightforward. First, you must order a credit report from each of the three credit bureaus. (There is a sample dispute letter included in this book that you can use as a template).

Second, when you receive the report, you will also receive a form to contest any negative items recorded on your report that are wrong.

Examples of how you might contest a notation are: “I was never 60 days late on this account”; “This account does not belong to me”; and “I do not owe this much to this creditor”, etc. The rules governing credit reporting state that you may not contest a negative item that is *accurate*, but you are entitled to have the correct information on your credit report. The trick is to find a legitimate way to contest the item. Then mail the form back to the credit reporting bureaus.

Once the negative item is contested, the credit reporting bureau has 30 days to attempt to verify the information. If they are able to contact the creditor, they will either update the report to accurately reflect the information, or they will delete the item if it was improperly listed. If they are unable to verify the data within the 30 days, the item must be removed from your record. Occasionally the debt has been sold or the creditor has gone out of business and the data cannot be confirmed. In other cases, the data is too old for the creditor to have any record of it, or perhaps it is in storage and is too difficult to access. In any case, it must come be removed if it cannot be verified.

You have probably seen ads about “credit wash” type companies. This is what they help you do. Many of these companies (not all) are not very reputable because they ask you to contest items that you *know* are correct. This is dangerous business, since it can be a crime. By doing this on your own, and contesting only those items you can legitimately contest, you will be surprised how much will come off your report. Also, for those items that they say were verified, but that you know are wrong, you can contest the charges once every 90 days. What the credit wash companies do well is mark your calendar and resubmit the contested items every 90 days. Surprisingly, items that were verified before will often come off on the second or third attempt.

The other approach, which you can do simultaneously, is to contact the creditor directly and ask them to update your report. Do this in writing, and keep a copy. Sometimes a creditor will remove a negative item just because you ask them to. I once had a 90-day late notation on my credit report for my student loan. I ended up paying it off early and asked them if they would please remove the 90-day late notation. To my surprise, they did!

One other criteria creditors use in determining your credit worthiness is the number of credit accounts that you have open. If you have too many open, the creditor is less likely to lend you money, because they fear you could get yourself in a lot of debt fast and become unable to repay them.

As a rule of thumb, you want about 3-5 credit accounts, not counting your car or your home. Over the years, you may have opened more credit accounts than you think. For example, let's say you bought a TV at Best Buy and you financed it with a "6 months same as cash" special offer. Let's also assume that you paid it off as agreed (it does not matter whether it was paid within the six months or not).

You may think that account is closed because it has a zero balance and you no longer get statements on it. You would be wrong. In most cases the account will reflect as an "open" account and hurt the possibility of obtaining new credit. So what do you do? You contest the account on the contest form by noting "This account has been closed." (You may have to call the original creditor and actually close the account by phone). Close all accounts that you have no use for.

There is hope! You can get your credit rating rebuilt. However, you should not be too anxious to rebuild your credit, because that was probably what got you into trouble in the first place… spending money that you did not have. At this stage, more than anything else, you need to develop the mindset of only buying those things that you can pay for with cash. You secure a certain peace of mind when you only spend what you earn and do not work merely to pay all the monthly bills. You must rethink your whole approach to money.

As often happens, you still need some credit to be able to do certain things, and there is a way to rebuild it. Keep in mind that rebuilding credit means rebuilding creditor confidence in your ability to pay bills. You must meet all your obligations promptly if you hope to obtain the good credit status you once had. It should go without saying that any accounts that remain open after the bankruptcy, such as your car or home loans, must remain current. This is crucial.

Assuming you are current or that you do not have a car loan, mortgage, or other secured loan that survived the bankruptcy, utilize the following 12 steps to get your good credit back:

THE 12 STEPS

1. Find a bank or a credit union - usually one that you have no previous banking relationship with, and open a savings account at the bank.

2. When you have saved $400 in the account, approach the bank officer about borrowing $300, using your savings account as collateral.

3. When you talk to the banker, be honest about your credit history and the filing of your bankruptcy. Explain that you are trying to rebuild your credit.

4. Usually you will be given the loan because the bank does not have any risk. You will probably be charged the highest interest rate allowed by law, and if you fail to pay, the bank can take your savings account.

5. After the loan is approved, do the same thing at another bank or credit union. Make the loan payments several days in advance of the date they are due.

6. When the loans are paid off, ask for larger loans. You will have demonstrated to the bank or credit union that you are a good customer and worthy of a riskier loan.

7. At this point you should be able to use the bank to finance future purchases like a jewelry, furniture, or cars. You can use the bank or credit union as a good credit reference.

8. When you have been paying on your loan for several months, contact the three credit bureaus to make sure that they have a history of your new credit. If they do not, ask the bank or credit union to supply the information. The credit reporting bureau will then add the information to your credit file.

   The credit bureaus are; Experian www.experian.com , P.O. Box 2104, Allen, TX 75013-2104; Equifax www.equifax.com , PO Box 740241, Atlanta, GA 30374-0241; and Trans Union www.transunion.com PO Box 390, Springfield, P A 19064-0390.

9. Next, apply for a national credit card (like Discover, Visa, or MasterCard).

10. If you do not qualify for an unsecured card, apply for a secured credit card, using the same principles as listed above. You can use a secured card just like a regular card, but you have to pledge some collateral for it, like your savings. You will find that as you make timely payments for six months, they will raise your credit substantially because they know that you cannot re-file a Chapter 7 for 8 years and that you have no other bills.

11. Never be late on your payments!

12. See number 11 above.

Your success in obtaining new credit is directly impacted by your ability to convince creditors that you are now a worthy credit risk. Prove this by paying your obligations on time, by showing a stable employment situation, and by making larger than necessary down payments on purchases.

Using my 12-Step method is the best way to rebuild your credit. Once you are on your feet again, use credit sparingly and wisely. Remember, it is a tool of convenience, but a very dangerous one. Do not let debt become a burden.

For further reading, I suggest *Credit after Bankruptcy*, 2008 edition, by Stephan Snyder and *Rich Dad, Poor Dad*, by Robert T. Kiyosaki.

You can find these on Amazon.com or get them for free at your local library by going to www.worldcat.org

Sample letter to be used for each credit reporting bureau

NOTE: *All letters should be sent by certified mail.*

Attention Equifax:

The following item has been incorrectly listed on my credit report:

Master Card Account xxxx-xxxx-xxxx-xxxx. Balance $xxx.xx.

The aforementioned debt was incurred prior to my Chapter 7 bankruptcy, case # xx-xxxxx-xxx. My case was discharged on xx/xx/xxxx. (See attached Discharge Notice).

Please reflect said item as discharged in bankruptcy on my credit report.

Thank you,

____

(Full Legal Name) (Date)

Conclusion and Disclaimer

I hope that you have enjoyed *The Bankruptcy Guide*. If you have questions, don't be alarmed. That is a good thing. This guide is designed to give you a better understanding of the issues surrounding bankruptcy law in 2012, but is in no way designed to be a substitute for proper legal counsel. If anything, I hope this guide has helped you understand what it is your lawyer will do for you. Simply put, a good lawyer is going to cut through the confusion and stress of the process and help you navigate your financial hardship in the least stressful and damaging way.

Best of luck,

Benjamin C. Yablon
Attorney at Law
1444 Stuart St.
Denver, CO 80204

Disclaimer: Nothing in this guide is intended to provide legal advice. Bankruptcy is complex, and even in the simplest cases you should consult an attorney.

Made in United States
Troutdale, OR
11/03/2026

56847373R00056